Discover Planets

Discover Uranus

Georgia Beth

Lerner Publications ◆ Minneapolis

Lerner Publications Company
A division of Lerner Publishing Group, Inc.
241 First Avenue North
Minneapolis, MN 55401 USA

For reading levels and more information, look up this title at www.lernerbooks.com.

Main body text set in Adrianna Regular 14/20.
Typeface provided by Chank.

Library of Congress Cataloging-in-Publication Data

Names: Beth, Georgia, author.
Title: Discover Uranus / Georgia Beth.
Description: Minneapolis: Lerner Publications, [2018] | Series: Searchlight books.
    Discover planets | Audience: Ages 8–11. | Audience: Grades 4 to 6. | Includes
    bibliographical references and index.
Identifiers: LCCN 2017058428 (print) | LCCN 2017056670 (ebook) |
    ISBN 9781541525474 (eb pdf) | ISBN 9781541523425 (lb : alk. paper) |
    ISBN 9781541527904 (pb : alk. paper)
Subjects: LCSH: Uranus (Planet)—Juvenile literature.
Classification: LCC QB681 (print) | LCC QB681 .B48 2018 (ebook) | DDC 523.47—dc23

LC record available at https://lccn.loc.gov/2017058428

Manufactured in the United States of America
1-44415-34674-3/26/2018

Contents

Chapter 1

A DISTANT NEIGHBOR

Far away, beyond the moon, Mars, Jupiter, and Saturn, there is a cold, dark region. Sunlight takes more than

two hours to reach there. This is where the mysterious world known as Uranus spins. Uranus is the seventh planet from the sun. Through a telescope, Uranus looks like a small, pale blue dot.

Uranus is named for the Greek god of the sky.

Against a dark sky, you can see Uranus with the naked eye.

Because Uranus is so far away from Earth, we don't know as much about it as we do about the planets in our solar system that are closer to Earth. But that hasn't stopped astronomers from asking questions.

How did Uranus form? Why does it look the way it does? What is it made of? Scientists don't have the answers to all of their questions yet. But they have learned a lot by studying Uranus through telescopes and by sending a probe to outer space.

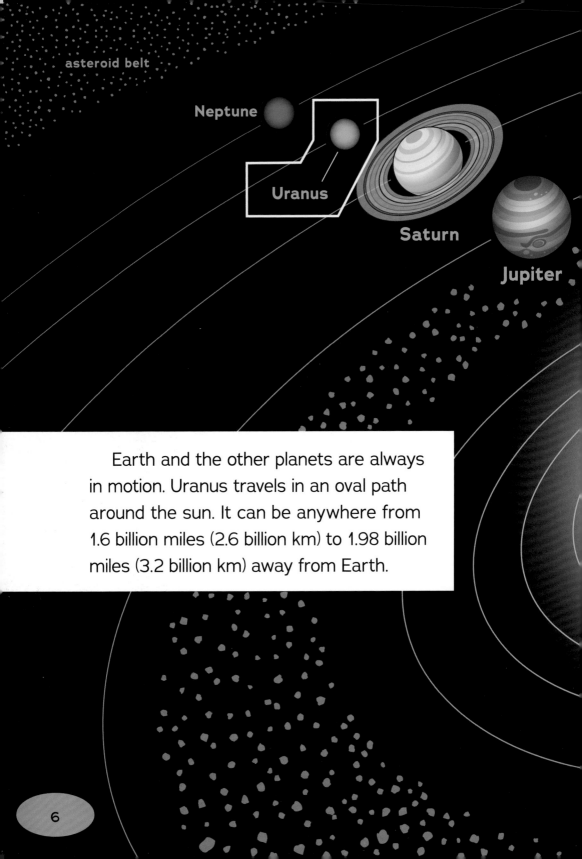

asteroid belt

Neptune

Uranus

Saturn

Jupiter

Earth and the other planets are always in motion. Uranus travels in an oval path around the sun. It can be anywhere from 1.6 billion miles (2.6 billion km) to 1.98 billion miles (3.2 billion km) away from Earth.

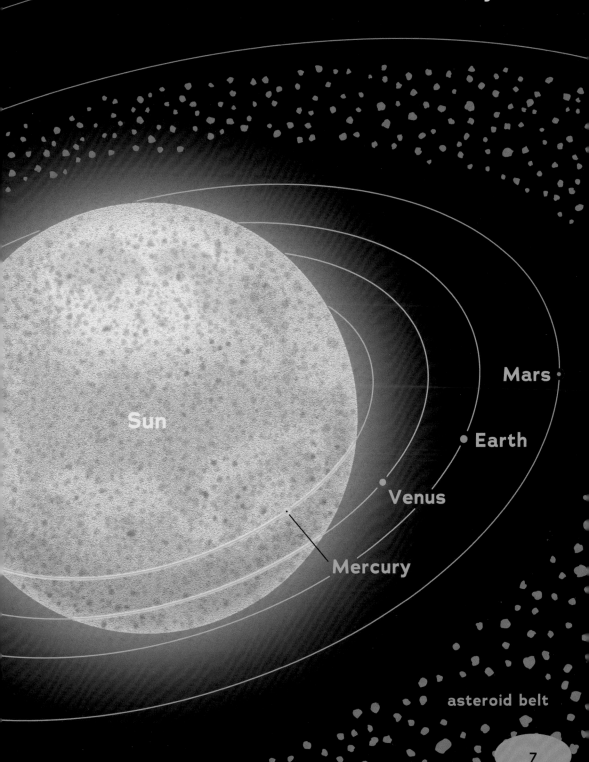

The Solar System

Mars

Earth

Sun

Venus

Mercury

asteroid belt

STEM Highlight

Scientists are curious people. When they don't have enough money to do research, they may reach out to amateurs, or people who take part in an activity for fun rather than as their job or for pay. Astronomer Heidi B. Hammel wanted to learn more about a bright spot seen on Uranus. She asked people with large telescopes to help. They looked at Uranus and shared images they'd taken of the bright spot. The images encouraged scientists to point the giant Hubble Space Telescope at Uranus and take a closer look!

Hammel is a research scientist at the Space Science Institute in Colorado.

Chapter 2

THE SIDEWAYS PLANET

Every planet spins around an axis, an invisible line that cuts through the center of each planet. Most planets spin counterclockwise at the same angle as the sun. But Uranus's axis is tipped on its side. The planet rotates clockwise at nearly a right angle to the sun.

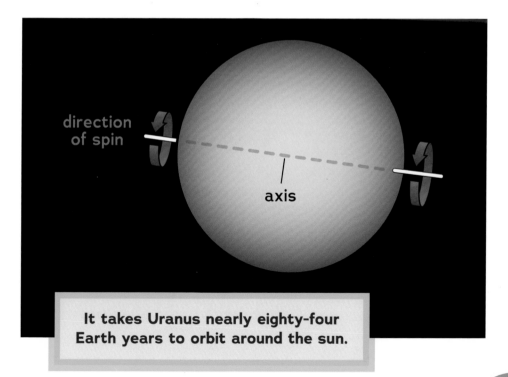

direction of spin

axis

It takes Uranus nearly eighty-four Earth years to orbit around the sun.

Uranus is almost four times wider than Earth.

A day on Uranus is about seventeen hours long. The planet's strange tilt causes extreme seasons. In winter, night lasts twenty-one Earth years, as half the planet is plunged into darkness. On the opposite side of the planet, summer means twenty-one Earth years of sunshine.

The atmosphere on Uranus is made up of thick clouds of hydrogen, helium, and methane. The probe that flew by Uranus could view only the top layer of the atmosphere. Scientists believe oceans may make up two-thirds of the planet.

Inside the planet, there is likely a small rocky core covered by a thick, slushy layer of ice and water. But most of the planet is a swirl of fluids.

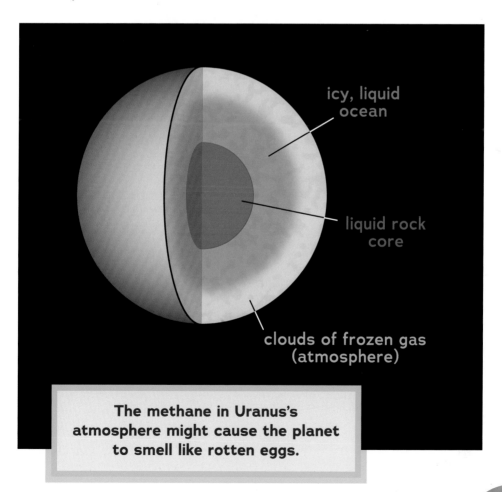

icy, liquid ocean

liquid rock core

clouds of frozen gas (atmosphere)

The methane in Uranus's atmosphere might cause the planet to smell like rotten eggs.

It would be impossible to land on Uranus. But if you could somehow hover close to the planet's surface, the first thing you might notice is how intensely cold it is. Temperatures on this planet are often near -357°F (-216°C). Winds can reach 560 miles (900 km) per hour. Huge storms roll through.

Ice in the clouds on Uranus reflect light so brightly that the storms can even be seen from Earth.

The moons of many of our planets are named after people from Greek myths, but most of Uranus's moons are named after characters from Shakespeare plays.

Many Moons

Twenty-seven moons orbit Uranus. There may also be two small moonlets that are so close to the planet they are difficult to see. The moons appear to be a mixture of frozen water and rock.

The moon Miranda looks like a puzzle whose pieces don't fit together properly. The moon has a mishmash of canyons, rough patches, and craters covered with ice. This moon is also home to Verona Rupes, the tallest cliff in the solar system.

Rings Revealed

Two sets of rings surround the planet. Scientists discovered them in 1977 when Uranus passed in front of a star and blocked the starlight. The inner set includes nine narrow, dark gray rings. The outer rings are bright red and blue. They seem to be made of ice, rocks, and other materials. Belts of fine dust float through the rings as well.

SCIENTISTS HAVE COUNTED A TOTAL OF THIRTEEN RINGS AROUND URANUS.

STEM Highlight

Uranus is known as an ice giant, although it's actually more liquid than solid. On Earth, the word *ice* refers to frozen water. But when astronomers use the word *ice*, they mean methane, water, and ammonia that may or may not be frozen. These are the main materials found on Uranus. Because of this, astronomers say Uranus is icy.

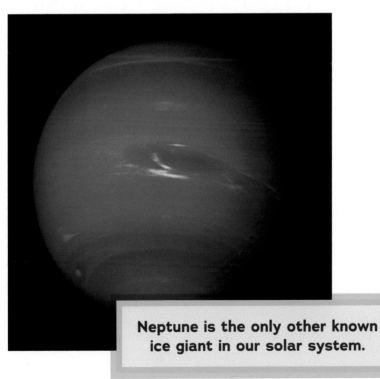

Neptune is the only other known ice giant in our solar system.

Chapter 3

RARE GLIMPSES

Learning about Uranus has been a slow process, and it's likely there's still much to discover. Uranus was the first planet discovered with a telescope. Astronomer William Herschel first saw the planet in 1781. But he originally thought it was a star. It took two years before scientists confirmed that Uranus was a planet.

William Herschel's sister Caroline often assisted him in his research.

Voyager 2 spent just six hours studying Uranus.

Voyager Mission

Much of what we know about Uranus comes from a single space mission. In the late 1970s, the planets aligned in a way that happens only once every 176 years. The US National Aeronautics and Space Administration (NASA) took advantage of this formation by designing a mission to explore Jupiter, Saturn, Uranus, and Neptune. The *Voyager 1* and *Voyager 2* probes were the first spacecraft to visit the farthest planets in our solar system. *Voyager 2* is the only probe that has flown by Uranus.

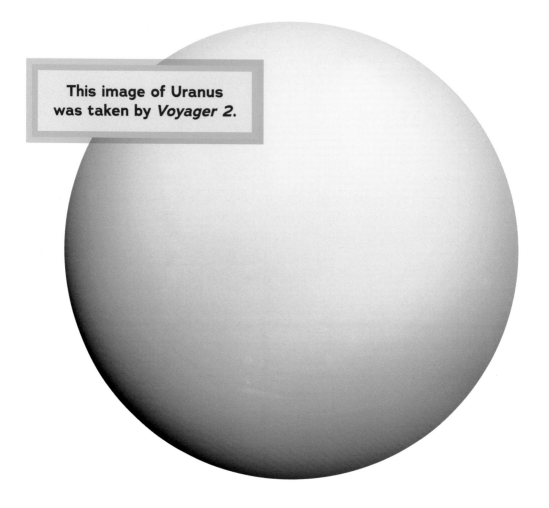

This image of Uranus was taken by *Voyager 2*.

Voyager 2 took pictures of Uranus and used instruments to measure the planet's atmosphere and temperature. It then sent this information to Earth. The information took about two and a half hours to reach Earth. There is four hundred times less light there than here on Earth, making it difficult to take clear photographs. Nevertheless, scientists have been studying the data for years.

STEM Highlight

Sunlight, as we see it, is colorless. But that visible light actually holds all the colors of the rainbow. When light from the sun hits an object, the object absorbs some colors and reflects the others. Our eyes see only the colors that are reflected. Objects absorb and reflect different colors depending on what they're made of.

The methane in Uranus's atmosphere absorbs red light. So our eyes see the green and blue light that's reflected. That's why the planet appears blue green even from far away.

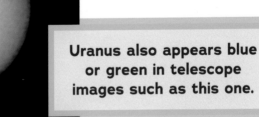

Uranus also appears blue or green in telescope images such as this one.

The Magnetic Field

Scientists learned the planet's strange tilt does more than cause intense weather. It affects the invisible magnetic field that surrounds the planet. Most planets with a magnetic field have clear north and south poles, just like here on

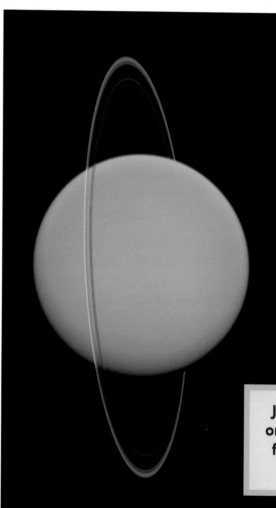

Earth. But because of the way Uranus's axis is tipped, the magnetic field is also tilted. The north and south poles aren't lined up with the top and bottom of the planet.

Just like the magnets on refrigerators have a field around them, so do many planets.

Chapter 4

TAKING ANOTHER LOOK

Scientists are still uncovering Uranus's secrets. And they're eager to learn more. While we've visited the planet only once, we have been watching closely from here on Earth.

Astronomers and researchers use large telescopes, such as the Hale Telescope, to view planets and other objects in space.

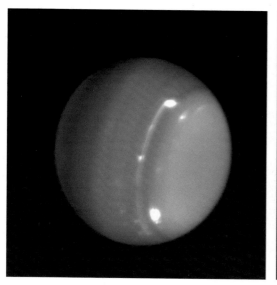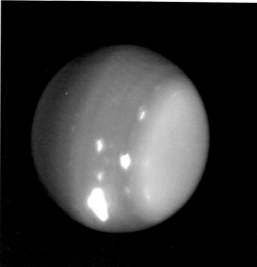

THESE IMAGES OF STORMS ON URANUS WERE TAKEN THROUGH A TELESCOPE AT THE W. M. KECK OBSERVATORY.

The W. M. Keck Observatory in Hawaii is home to some of the biggest telescopes on Earth. Scientists at the observatory often observe Uranus. Astronomers have seen strong storms in the planet's clouds. One intense storm appeared to produce 30 percent of all the light reflected from the planet!

The Hubble Space Telescope orbits Earth. It lets astronomers see stars and planets more clearly and in greater detail than telescopes on Earth. The Hubble Telescope made many of the most recent discoveries about Uranus.

The telescopes at the W. M. Keck Observatory and the Hubble Telescope often work together so scientists can be sure about what they're seeing. In 2005, both sets of telescopes confirmed Uranus's outermost ring is blue and the next ring is red.

The Hubble Telescope has made more than 1.3 million observations since it was launched into orbit in 1990.

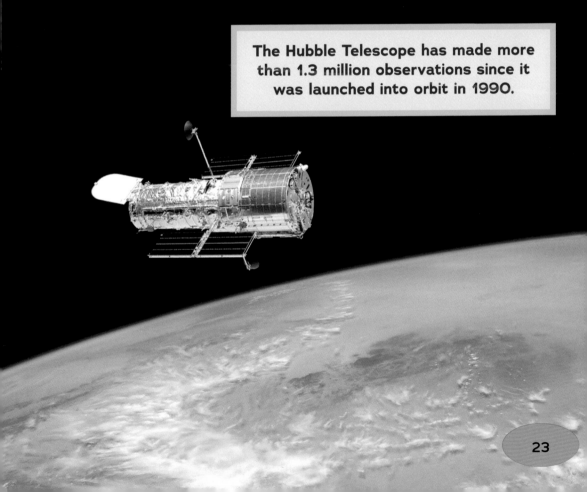

Modern computers are more powerful than those scientists used in the 1980s to study data from *Voyager 2*. Scientists are still studying the images. They expected all the clouds in Uranus's atmosphere to move around the planet at similar speeds. But it appears that the southern areas of the planet's atmosphere are rotating faster than the northern areas. Astronomers think some strange part of the planet's interior may cause the difference in how the clouds move.

Some scientists think the clouds at Uranus's north pole (*on the planet's right side in this image*) look like popcorn.

An artist created this image of *New Horizons* orbiting Pluto.

Returning to Uranus

In 2011, a probe called *New Horizons* passed Uranus on its way to Pluto, but the probe was mostly inactive until it reached Pluto, so it was unable to collect any data of Uranus.

Curiosity drives us to explore. But time and money are limited. We can explore only a few places at once. In the near future, Uranus may be one of those places on NASA's list.

The James Webb Space Telescope is being built to help astronomers observe distant planets and other objects.

In 2017, NASA announced that it may send a probe to Uranus again. It would be part of a mission to study the ice giants. Scientists hope to better understand the solar system and learn more about how planets form and change. Part of NASA's plan includes designing new technology for the missions.

Ice giants are unknown to us. But they appear to be common outside of our solar system. Learning more about the distant planets in our solar system may help us explore even more distant places. Scientists hope to send a probe out to Uranus in the next twenty years.

WHO KNOWS WHAT WE WILL LEARN ABOUT URANUS DURING THE NEXT MISSION?

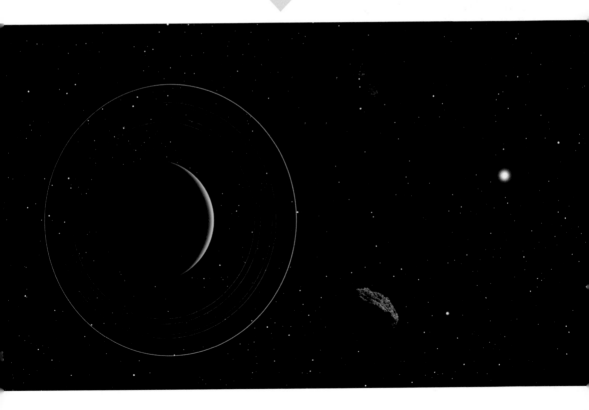

STEM Highlight

Nearly every planet in the solar system has auroras, including Uranus. Auroras are broad bands of light that appear in the sky. When an aurora occurs at Earth's North Pole, it is called the northern lights. Auroras occur when tiny pieces in the magnetic field collide with the atmosphere, causing them to give off light. On Earth, tiny pieces in the sun's solar wind cause the auroras. This wind affects Uranus in the same way, even though the planet is nearly 2 billion miles (3.2 billion km) away. Even more amazing, the shimmering lights appear to rotate with the planet.

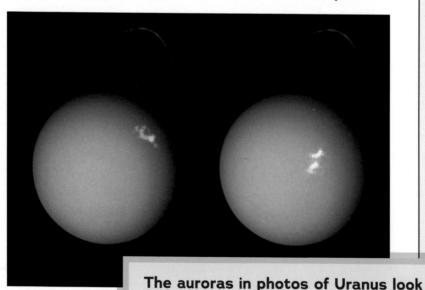

The auroras in photos of Uranus look like glowing dots or patchy spots.

Looking Ahead

- Because telescopes and *Voyager 2* have only seen Uranus's atmosphere, 99 percent of the planet remains to be explored.

- Scientists have discovered an ice giant similar to Uranus 25,000 light-years away. They're studying the distant planet in hopes of learning more about Uranus.

- Telescopes are able to view the edges of Uranus's rings only every forty-two years. Recent images taken by the telescopes showed meteorites may be causing the rings to change shape. Scientists hope to continue to learn more about the rings.

Glossary

angle: the direction in which something is sloped

astronomer: a person who studies objects and forces outside Earth's atmosphere, such as planets, stars, and energy traveling through space

atmosphere: the gases that surround a planet

core: the central part of a planet

data: facts about something or information in number form that can be used to calculate, reason, or plan

fluid: a substance such as a liquid or gas that flows or takes the shape of a container

magnetic field: the area around a magnetic object that carries an electric current that creates magnetic forces

orbit: to travel around another object in an oval or circular path

probe: a device that travels to and sends back information from outer space

solar system: a group consisting of a star and the planets and other objects that orbit the star. In our solar system, the star is called the sun.

solar wind: a steady flow of tiny energized pieces floating outward from the sun through the solar system

Learn More about Uranus

Books

Aguilar, David A. *Space Encyclopedia: A Tour of Our Solar System and Beyond*. Washington, DC: National Geographic, 2013. Tour the solar system with this reference book filled with full-color photographs and illustrations.

Goldstein, Margaret J. *Discover Neptune*. Minneapolis: Lerner Publications, 2019. Learn about Neptune, our solar system's other ice giant, in this book.

Taylor-Butler, Christine. *Planet Uranus*. New York: Children's Press, 2014. Read this book to learn more information about Uranus and its role in the solar system.

Websites

Mission to Uranus
https://kids.nationalgeographic.com/explore/space/mission-to -uranus/#uranus-planet.jpg
Check out this website and imagine what it would be like to travel on a mission to Uranus.

Uranus
https://www.brainpop.com/science/space/uranus/
Learn more about Uranus by watching a video, taking a quiz, making a mind map, and more at this fun website.

Uranus Facts
https://space-facts.com/uranus/
Visit this website to learn more fun facts about Uranus.

Index

Photo Acknowledgments

The images in this book are used with the permission of: Mark Garlick/Science Photo Library/Getty Images, p. 4; Photo Researchers/Getty Images, p. 5; Laura Westlund/Independent Picture Service, pp. 6–7, 9, 11; NASA/Bill Ingalls, p. 8; SCIEPRO/Science Photo Library/Getty Images, pp. 10, 20; NASA/JPL/USGS, p. 12; QAI Publishing/UIG/Getty Images, p. 13; courtesy of Seran Gibbard Lawrence Livermore National Laboratory, Imke de Pater of UC Berkeley, Mark Showalter of the SETI Institute and Heidi Hammel of the Space Science Institute, p. 14; NASA/JPL, pp. 15, 17; Universal History Archive/Getty Images, p. 16; NASA/JPL-Caltech, p. 18; NASA & ESA, p. 19; Joe McNally/Getty Images, p. 21; Imke De Pater (UC Berkeley)/Keck Observatory, p. 22; NASA, pp. 23, 25; courtesy of Lawrence Sromovsky, Pat Fry, Heidi Hammel, Imke de Pater, p. 24; NASA/Chris Gunn, p. 26; Stocktrek Images/Getty Images, p. 27; NASA, ESA, and L. Lamy (Observatory of Paris, CNRS, CNES), p. 28.

Cover: SCIEPRO/Getty Images.